SCHOLASTIC CANADA
BIOGRAPHY

MEET
Chris Hadfield

ELIZABETH
MACLEOD

ILLUSTRATED BY
MIKE DEAS

Scholastic Canada Ltd.
Toronto New York London Auckland Sydney
Mexico City New Delhi Hong Kong Buenos Aires

Gazing out the window of the International Space Station, Chris Hadfield grinned. He had wanted to be an astronaut since he was a kid. Chris had worked hard and trained for years. Now, on his third trip to space, he was in command of the mission.

When Chris was nine years old he saw an incredible sight. On July 20, 1969, Chris and his family were gathered with their neighbours around a television. All over the world, people tuned in to watch an astronaut walk on the moon for the very first time. Everyone cheered!

Chris couldn't stop thinking about what he'd seen. It was amazing. He began dreaming of being an astronaut.

It seemed impossible. Canada didn't even have a space program! But Chris wondered if someday it *might* be possible.

Chris and his family lived on a farm in Milton, Ontario. He liked knowing how things worked and learned how to fix the farm machinery.

Chris studied hard in school. When he was thirteen, he joined the Air Cadets. There, he learned about leadership and how to fly gliders.

6

After high school, Chris joined the Canadian Armed Forces. Many astronauts started their careers in the military. He went to military college and got a degree in mechanical engineering.

Chris trained as a fighter pilot after college. He patrolled Canada's northern skies, but he still dreamed of going to space.

Chris went on to become a test pilot. He worked hard and was usually at the top of his class. He tested new systems, including ones to help save F-18 fighters in out-of-control situations.

In 1983, six Canadians had been picked to train at the National Aeronautics and Space Administration (NASA) in Houston, Texas. Chris's dream of going to space seemed a little more possible.

ROBERTA BONDAR, MARC GARNEAU, ROBERT THIRSK, KEN MONEY, BJARNI TRYGGVASON, STEVE MACLEAN - - - MAYBE ME TOO ONE DAY?!

DEPARTURE FROM CONTROLLED FLIGHT ESTABLISHED, BEGINNING TEST SEQUENCE NOW.

Nine years later, Canada announced it was hiring more astronauts. Chris was ready! He sent in his application right away. More than 5000 people applied.

For months, Chris took tests, attended meetings and answered questions. Then he waited for the results. And waited. Would he get a chance to be an astronaut?

SO TELL US WHAT YOU WOULD DO IN THAT KIND OF EMERGENCY.

On June 8, 1992, Chris was chosen as one of Canada's four new astronauts. His first trip to space would take place in 1995. Chris would fly on a space shuttle to Mir, the Russian space station. Chris spent three years at NASA practising the systems he'd be using in space and learning to speak Russian.

On November 12, 1995, the shuttle lifted off and roared toward space. A few minutes later, Chris realized his face was sore. Was something wrong? No — he was smiling so much that he had cramps in his cheeks!

Chris was a mission specialist and part of his role was to operate the Canadarm. This series of jointed robotic arms was invented in Canada. It could grab satellites or spacecraft, make repairs and move supplies or even astronauts.

Chris had practised simulations, or "sims," with the Canadarm many times in his training. He was ready, and did his job well.

Chris returned to Earth after eight days. He had loved being on the space station.

In 1997, Chris found out he'd be heading back into space. This time he was flying to the new International Space Station (ISS).

The first section of the ISS went into orbit in 1998. It would take twelve years and forty missions to transport all the sections of the ISS into space and assemble them.

Chris and the other astronauts would arrive at the ISS in April 2001. They would help build new parts of it. That meant Chris would need to go outside the ISS and walk in space.

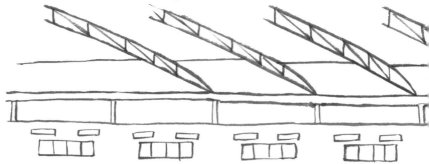

Underwater is the closest we can get on Earth to the microgravity of space. Before a spacewalk, astronauts train in a huge swimming pool. They wear special suits carefully weighted so they don't float or sink. Pants, tops, gloves, helmets — everything has to be watertight.

It takes hours for astronauts to assemble their tools, discuss the day's training and get helped into the bulky suits. Then they are lowered on a platform into the pool.

IT'S HARDER TO DO THIS UNDERWATER THAN ON LAND. IT'S GOOD WE PRACTISE OVER AND OVER.

On April 22, 2001, Chris stepped out of the ISS. He was the first Canadian to walk in space. Chris and his partner's job was to install Canadarm2 on the ISS. The Canadarm2 is a larger, more advanced version of the robotic arm Chris used on the Mir mission.

Everything was going well until Chris suddenly got something in his eyes. They stung so much he couldn't open them. He was blind in space!

No one knew what was wrong. Mission Control back on Earth told Chris to open a valve in his suit to vent the suit's air into space. Fresh air would be pumped into the suit from the tanks.

YES. WE CAN MOVE ON TO THE NEXT ONE.

HAVE YOU GOT THAT BOLT TIGHTENED?

Endeavour

Chris kept calm, and slowly his eyes cleared. He was finally able to get back to work. Chris and his partner were out in space for more than seven hours. The rest of the work went according to plan.

Later, NASA figured out that some of the liquid used to clean the visor on Chris's helmet had gotten into his eyes. Now they use different cleaners.

Just two days after his first spacewalk — which astronauts call an extravehicular activity, or EVA — Chris left the ISS for his second. He cleaned his visor very carefully this time!

During the EVA, Chris and his partner removed an old communications antenna from the ISS. They also moved equipment from the shuttle to a storage rack on one of the space station's labs.

A week later, it was time for Chris to return home.

IT'S LIKE EARTH IS A SHIP AND WE'RE ALL TRAVELLING THROUGH SPACE TOGETHER - - -

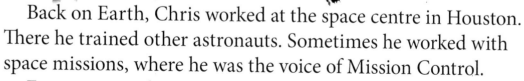

Back on Earth, Chris worked at the space centre in Houston. There he trained other astronauts. Sometimes he worked with space missions, where he was the voice of Mission Control.

For two years, he was NASA's Director of Operations in Russia. He learned more about the Russian space systems and the cosmonauts — that's the Russian term for astronauts.

Chris loved his work. But he wondered if he'd ever get to go to space again.

Chris had to wait many years, but in 2010 he found out he'd been chosen to go back to the ISS for 146 days — and this time he would be in command!

Chris knew he'd have to be totally prepared for this space mission. He would be responsible for the safety of the people on board and the station itself. Chris and his crew took two years to get ready for their mission.

On December 19, 2012, Chris and his two teammates prepared to blast off on the Russian Soyuz spacecraft to the ISS.

It was very cold. To make sure they didn't freeze on their way to the launch pad, they wore pillowy snowsuits over their spacesuits. They waddled as they walked.

As Chris climbed the stairs to the Soyuz, he noticed it was covered in ice. But the spacecraft easily rocketed them to the ISS.

19

THE SOYUZ DOCKING PROBE IS ALIGNED FOR THE FINAL APPROACH.

Before astronauts arrive at the ISS, they train inside three-dimensional models of the space station. That way, when they come on board, they are prepared to get to work.

The ISS is a solar-powered research lab that orbits around Earth. It was developed by the United States, Europe, Japan, Russia and Canada. Usually it has a crew of six.

The ISS is the biggest spacecraft ever created and it cost more than $120 billion to build. It is made up of connected tubes and compartments where the astronauts live and work.

By 2013, the ISS was as long as a football field. Sometimes for fun, the crew would have races from one end to the other, pushing off the walls and flying through the tubes.

Most of the food on the ISS is dry and in bags. Astronauts squirt water into the food, then mix it up and eat it right out of the bag.

Gravity is the force that keeps you on the ground. Astronauts don't feel gravity in space. This is tough on their bodies. Their muscles can become weak. To stay healthy, they work out for two hours every day.

There is no running water on the station. When the crew brushes their teeth, they have to swallow the toothpaste.

The ISS toilet is a small booth. There's a long hose coming out of the wall that sucks the waste away. But a few drops always escape. Each astronaut is careful to wipe the walls clean after.

Chris and the crew kept busy checking that the equipment on the ISS was working properly. They also did experiments. They tested how their hearts were working and grew plants in space.

But Chris wanted to get people on Earth excited about space. Answering questions from schools and reporters and posting photos to Twitter were just some of the ways Chris helped people learn about space. He shared more than 100 videos from the ISS!

Chris loves playing the guitar. There was one on board the ISS. He sang "Is Somebody Singing" live with kids all across Canada.

Chris also recorded a video of "Space Oddity" by rock superstar David Bowie. It was the first music video made in space. Millions of people on Earth watched it.

People liked seeing the world through an astronaut's eyes. Chris showed them how beautiful and amazing space is.

Chris's 146-day mission was going well. It was almost over. Then one of the astronauts saw sparks flying from the side of the ISS. What was happening?

Mission Control back on Earth said the space station was leaking a chemical called ammonia that keeps the station's power systems from getting too hot. This was very serious. There was no time to run any sims for the repair.

THE NEW PUMP IS IN AND THERE'S NO SIGN OF A LEAK.

Two astronauts had to go out and fix the leak. As ISS commander, Chris stayed on board to coach them.

Chris worked with Mission Control to direct the repairs, speaking both Russian and English. He stayed calm and took the astronauts through everything they needed to do.

It took them more than five hours to stop the leak. But with Chris's help, they did it. The ISS and its crew were safe.

27

BOY, THAT WAS QUITE A RIDE!

Chris returned safely to Earth on May 13, 2013. Thanks to his songs, tweets, pictures and videos, he became one of the most famous astronauts ever.

Later that year, Chris retired from being an astronaut. He wrote books, including one for kids.

Today, Chris travels around the world. He gives talks about what it's like to be an astronaut. He shares stories about the everyday things that are weird in space. By helping people see the world differently, he hopes they'll see its wonder.

In his talks, Chris also reminds people that to reach your goals, you need to work hard and be prepared, so that you will be ready for whatever adventures are ahead. Just like Chris!

Chris Hadfield's Life

August 29, 1959	Chris Austin Hadfield is born in Sarnia, Ontario.
July 20, 1969	Chris watches the first moon landing on television.
1978	Chris joins the Canadian Armed Forces.
1982	Chris graduates from the Royal Military College in Kingston, Ontario, with an engineering degree.
Late 1980s	Chris attends test pilot school and works as a professional test pilot in the United States.
June 8, 1992	Chris is chosen to be an astronaut.
November 12–20, 1995	Chris makes his first space flight. He flies to Russia's Mir space station on mission STS-74. Chris is the only Canadian to have gone on a mission to Mir.
April 19–May 1, 2001	Chris's second mission to space. He flies to the International Space Station on mission STS-100.

CHRIS, AGE 5.

CHRIS WORKS ON ATTACHING THE CANADARM2 TO THE OUTSIDE OF THE INTERNATIONAL SPACE STATION DURING HIS FIRST SPACEWALK, ON APRIL 22, 2001.

April 22, 2001	Chris becomes the first Canadian to walk in space.
2001–2003	Chris is NASA's Director of Operations in Russia
December 19, 2012	Chris leaves for his third trip to space, Expedition 34/35.
March 13–May 13, 2013	Chris is the first Canadian to be commander of the ISS.
May 12, 2013	Chris is the first person ever to record and broadcast a music video from space.
July 3, 2013	Chris retires from the Canadian Space Agency.
November 18, 2015	Chris is becomes an Officer of the Order of Canada.
September 10, 2016	*The Darkest Dark,* Chris's first picture book, is published.

THIS STAMP WAS ISSUED AS PART OF A 2003 SERIES HONOURING CANADIAN ASTRONAUTS AND CANADA'S ACHIEVEMENTS IN SPACE.

LIVE FROM SPACE VIA VIDEO LINK-UP, CHRIS DOES A QUESTION AND ANSWER SESSION WITH STUDENTS AT CHRIS HADFIELD ELEMENTARY SCHOOL IN MILTON, ONTARIO.

*With lots of love for my great-nephews Colwyn
and Tennyson Rich. The sky's the limit
for all you can achieve!*

— E.M.

For all our future astronauts!

— M.D.

Many thanks to editor Erin O'Connor for helping this book lift off!
Thanks also to the whole team at Scholastic, especially the book's
illustrator, Mike Deas. I'm very grateful to Chris Hadfield for
reviewing the book. Thanks also to my brothers, John and Douglas.
Special thanks to Paul for "flying me to the moon . . ."

— E.M.

Scholastic Canada Ltd.
604 King Street West, Toronto, Ontario M5V 1E1, Canada

Scholastic Inc.
557 Broadway, New York, NY 10012, USA

Scholastic Australia Pty Limited
PO Box 579, Gosford, NSW 2250, Australia

Scholastic New Zealand Limited
Private Bag 94407, Botany, Manukau 2163, New Zealand

Scholastic Children's Books
Euston House, 24 Eversholt Street, London NW1 1DB, UK

www.scholastic.ca

The illustrations were created using a blend of digital tools with traditional media.
Sketches were created with a Wacom tablet and Photoshop, then traced onto watercolour
paper, where colour and texture were added using gouache and watercolour paints.
Ink was used to add the black line to finish the art.

Photos ©: cover and title page speech bubble, top right: fatmayilmaz/iStockphoto;
30 left: Courtesy Chris Hadfield; 30 right: NASA; 31 left: Courtesy Canada Post;
31 right: Richard Lautens/Toronto Star/Getty Images.

Library and Archives Canada Cataloguing in Publication

MacLeod, Elizabeth, author
    Meet Chris Hadfield / Elizabeth MacLeod ; illustrated by Mike Deas.

(Scholastic Canada biography)
ISBN 978-1-4431-1947-4 (softcover).--ISBN 978-1-4431-6389-7 (hardcover)

    1. Hadfield, Chris, 1959- --Juvenile literature. 2. Astronauts--
Canada--Biography--Juvenile literature. 3. Biographies.
I. Deas, Mike, 1982-, illustrator II. Title.

TL789.85.H34M34 2018   j629.450092   C2017-907350-8

6 5 4 3 2 1   Printed in Malaysia 108   18 19 20 21 22